D1498489

THREE WORDS AND A KISS

A Guide for Effective Self-Leadership

Todd Wright

©Better Legacy Books

DEDICATION:

To my six grandchildren, Clark (age 6), Boaz (age 5), Hank (age 4), Ada (age 3), Walt (age 2), and Willa (age 1), I dedicate this book to you.

I believe in you and expect great things from your voyage. Life is a gift from God. Live yours to honor HIM, bless others, and make the world better than you found it. May the stories and principles in this book bring you as much joy, perspective, and inspiration as you have brought me. And through these pages, may my voice continue to speak wisdom and guidance into your lives long after I am gone.

Enjoy the journey!

I love you!

Papaw Todd Wright
2022

If you have ever known the joy of sitting on a front-porch in rural America listening to a witty and wise old sage, you're going to love Three Words and a Kiss. Author Todd Wright delivers vital lessons for effective self-leadership that will make you better, lessons you'll not soon forget. He dares us to dream because, as he says, "You can change the world with a great dream, but you can hardly change your socks without one." This is likely the best book you'll read this year!

-Roger Alford, Editor, The Christian Index

CONTENTS

FOREWORD

When I hear the name Todd Wright, the words *legacy leadership* come to mind. I see a leader who consistently exhibits the qualities of strength and compassion. His life's investment is not limited to members of the church he leads, stretching to countless others all over the globe. It is very difficult in today's climate to find a leader who both talks the talk and walks the walk. The credibility of Todd's own self-leadership helps solidify these truths. Simply put, this book will leave an impact on your life!

If you are developing new leadership skills or just wanting to broaden your perspective, you will get that in this book - a lasting impact. Too often leadership principles get lost in their own complexity of wordy content, but here we have simple truths embedded in great stories. Having spent over 30 years of my life serving what I believe to be one of the world's greatest companies, Chick-fil-A, leadership is at the forefront of everything we do. The values and principles expressed in this book, *Three Words and a Kiss*, parallel so much of what we believe in our organization.

As a student of leadership, I can appreciate the impact that real life stories have on the development of a leader. Todd, in his own unique way, brings to life wise precepts through the power of story. As you begin this journey with him, lean in, take good notes, and be prepared to sharpen your skills as a leader.

David Daniels
Chick-fil-A, Owner and Operator

PREFACE

The seeds of thought for this book began in 1991, as I typed out one of the stories inside and jotted down a couple of lessons I had learned from it. That was over 30 years ago. I often went several years without writing anything, and then a burst of inspiration would lead me to script another story that influenced my life in a significant way.

Until a few years ago, I never thought it appropriate for these writings to become a book for public consumption, as they were deeply personal and showed a level of vulnerability. In my mind, it was a mixture of memories and practical wisdom my children and grandchildren would read after I died. It was my way of speaking into their lives and cheering for their success long after I'm gone. As the years went by, more experiences, people, and lessons from my past made it to the forefront of my thoughts and onto these pages. Then in the spring of 2017, the dream of a book began to form inside me. My writings had a common theme of self-leadership. Moreover, they were not just my stories for my family, but they were stories of the human experience as we attempt to lead ourselves toward the best life possible.

The title, THREE WORDS AND A KISS, came from an experience I had with my Papaw Bentley as he taught me how to plow with a mule when I was just a kid. "Gee" told the mule to go right. "Haw" meant go left. "Whoa" meant stop. A kissing sound told the mule to go forward. Leading the massive four-legged creature was simple and easy. I could lead the mule effectively with just three words and a kiss. As I grew older, I realized much more effort would be required to effectively lead myself.

My approach to self-leadership here may draw criticism from Christian readers expecting a book filled with Christian lingo and Bible verses, since I am a pastor. I did not write it to an exclusively Christian audience, but from a simple human perspective to a broad human audience. Why? Because, low self-esteem, feelings of inadequacy, self-awareness, and self-sabotage are emotional growth and character issues and are not exclusive to any one group. They are challenges of all humanity. The churches I have led are filled with people who still feel inadequate, blame other people, get their feelings hurt, quit when times get tough, and sometimes behave as their own worst enemies. People with the same feelings also occupy the local jail, university, and corporate office. No doubt, my faith is the most impactful aspect of my life, and while it promises eternal life, it does not promise emotional growth. Like everyone else in the world who wants a better life, I must rise each day and lead myself to make good choices. With that said, thank you for choosing to get better by reading this book.

Joyfully,
Todd Wright

CHAPTER 1: SELF-LEADERSHIP REFLECTIONS

... they have no idea of the internal fight I face every day to embrace effective self-leadership.

The most powerful voice we hear each day is our own. We talk to ourselves about every challenge, dream, and decision we face. That inner voice is sometimes our greatest cheerleader, and at other times our worst critic. It either champions success or predicts failure. It escalates courage or intensifies fear. It controls the horizon of our future.

Should I give my best, or give up and quit? Can I do that, or can I not? Should I take responsibility, or blame someone else? Was I created on purpose and for a purpose, or is my life built on luck and chance? Should I quit, or dig deep and keep trying? Are my failures final, or can I move beyond them to succeed? These are just a few of the questions our inner voice attempts to answer, and it often gives us very bad advice. Even when it is good advice, we struggle to find the nerve to take action and move in the right direction. This is the concept of self-leadership.

Leadership in every situation is challenging, and leading ourselves is the most difficult of all; it is also the most important. Unless we master it, our future will be mundane and mediocre at best. At worst, a life of disappointment and disaster looms as each day ticks by. But... if we can learn to lead ourselves effectively, incredible days are ahead!

I know. I was once a shy, introverted kid who felt inadequate, inferior to everyone, afraid of failure and embarrassment. I was scared of saying the wrong thing, so I was silent in unfamiliar settings. I lived in the shadow of my three brothers, who were outstanding athletes. I was terrible at sports. They were physically fit and in great shape. I was round and plump. I also craved the approval and affirmation of others. I was an emotionally weak kid with a low self-esteem. All of these obstacles were inside of me, and I took them wherever I went. My inner voice spoke of my flaws and fears continually, at times, as a whisper, at others, it was a yell; but it was always there to speak a dark cloud of doubt over my future success. I needed to change the message, tone, and tenor of that voice if I would ever excel toward my potential. Thanks to some really special people who invested in me along the way, I learned. I grew. I changed. And my future became brighter.

A Successful Day

After much growth and many years later, it was one of those perfect spring days in Georgia, the kind that causes you to raise your face toward heaven and say, "thank you". The mid-morning sun shone from a cloudless sky. A warm, gentle breeze moved softly among a crowd of smiling, happy people making their way into the Coliseum at the University of West Georgia. This part of the state is home to me. Except for my first year as an infant, my entire childhood had been lived within thirty miles of the spot where I was standing. And several generations of my family lived their lives here before me. It is a place of countless happy memories, and this day would provide one more that would forever be etched in my mind.

I watched as grandfathers and grandmothers, moms and dads, infants and toddlers, children and teens and twenty-somethings – thousands of them – made their way toward the Coliseum. Some rode shuttles. Others strolled along sidewalks, relishing the 70-plus degree temperatures. Greeters stood at various places like human signposts, pointing people toward the entrances. There was a sense of fulfillment, anticipation, and expectation in the air. As my wife, Lisa, and I neared the entrance, we could hear music spilling through the doors. The band was completing last-minute sound checks.

The last time I had been to the Coliseum, a much younger me played on a basketball team of community leaders against the world-famous Harlem Globetrotters to raise funds for the Central High School band. We lost, of course, but the game was a huge win because it generated lots of money for the kids.

This day's event was no ballgame. It was a church service. Easter Sunday. The Coliseum would be filled with people from all walks of life coming together for what would be the largest crowd ever for Midway Church, where I served as pastor. To accommodate the Easter crowd in a single service, we had moved it to the larger venue at the university. We were expecting many more people than our thirteen-hundred seat sanctuary could accommodate, even with multiple services. And we certainly got them.

I was nervous. Thousands of eyes would be on me, and my voice would fill the cavernous building for over thirty minutes. As I got ready to take the stage, my thoughts went back to my childhood when the mere idea of speaking in front of even a small group struck paralyzing fear in my heart. I realized my palms had become sweaty, my heart thumped faster, and my mouth was unusually dry. My inner voice said, "This is a massive crowd. Your largest ever! Suppose you mess up?" Then a louder inner voice encouraged me, "You can do this!"

I listened to one last song transition from crescendo to silence. That was my cue. I stepped carefully and purposefully to the podium and told over four thousand people about the death, burial, and resurrection of Jesus Christ. I explained why we believe in the resurrection, why millions of people gather around the world every Easter to celebrate it, and why the resurrection matters. When I finished, people streamed forward to place their faith in Jesus. As a preacher, that's as good as it gets. It was a pinnacle experience for a small-town boy who had to learn to push himself beyond his limits, beyond his insecurities to achieve any level of success. Emotionally, I was fulfilled, ecstatic, and grateful.

Later that day, I was off to the airport for an overnight flight to Germany, to speak at an international leadership conference, to help people become better. I had grown accustomed to such trips. To date, I had served and trained leaders in 35 nations on five continents. These trips were great for me, too. They energized me. Traveling to distant lands and living among people from different cultures helped me keep life in focus. The downtime that came with being on a plane for long flights had it benefits. For me, the inside of a plane at 35,000 feet was an inspirational place, a place where my mind ran wild, where I could think, dream, reflect, plan, and solve problems.

As I traveled that night over the Atlantic Ocean, I reflected on the large crowd I had spoken to at the coliseum. It was a peak moment for me. I thought of the wonderful life I was able to experience, of the challenges I had overcome, and of the dreams I had seen evolve. I had dreamed of preaching to big crowds and that dream had become a reality. I had dreamed of marrying a blonde-headed girl who lived up the road and of building a life and family together. I did, and we are. Together, we had dreamed of having our own farm with horses and cattle. We have. I had dreamed of experiencing adventure, of traveling and seeing the world I read about in books. I do.

As a person of faith, I knew God is the source of every good thing in life, but He had not handed it to me on a silver platter. To reach my potential, He had taken me on a difficult journey of ups and downs to forge courage and strength into my fragile and weak character. He had required me to learn, change, and grow. I asked myself, "How did I get here? What experiences, places, and people had impacted me most? What had I learned? How had I learned?"

My mind drifted back to my childhood in the rolling foothills of the Appalachians. It was a much simpler time and place. The world as I knew it covered only a few square miles around Riverside Road, next to the Tallapoosa River in Tallapoosa, Georgia. A wonderful family surrounded me there, who loved me beyond measure and taught me everything I needed to know to lead a successful life.

Now, on this nine-hour flight, my thoughts took me back to those days growing up in small-town Georgia. I could hear Mamaw's voice from long ago, "Son, don't ever forget where you came from!" I never will. My parents and grandparents, along with some mentors and dedicated teachers, exposed me to seemingly simple life experiences that turned out to be transformational lessons. They became tools to improve my inner voice, and principles to carve out the life I now live. They have helped me fight through every challenge and conquer every fear, so I could excel and build a respectable life.

While other passengers on the plane slept, watched movies, or read, I was on a wooded hillside above the Tallapoosa River listening to my redbone hound chase a raccoon. I was feeding cattle with Papaw. I was helping customers in Mom and Dad's small store. I was sitting in a school classroom learning alongside my classmates. I was plowing corn behind a well-mannered mule. And I was feeling altogether fortunate for such an upbringing and for everything I had learned. My reflective thoughts of the experiences, people, places, and events of the past were good and refreshing for my soul as these lessons of life unfolded.

Reflecting About The Journey

I pondered. How did I grow beyond my youthful introversion and my feelings of inadequacy to become a pastor of thousands and an instructor at international leadership conferences? How had I gone from being a boy who felt great anxiety leaving his neighborhood to feeling perfectly at home traveling around the world? How did I grow from being insecure in basic conversation to speaking with confidence to large audiences?

As I moved from the stages of childhood, youthfulness, and early adulthood, my inner voice became wiser, kinder, and more beneficial to follow. At some point, my "self-talk" began to affirm me and my value in this world. It started cheering for my success and my personal confidence increased.

Even after I grew and matured emotionally, my inner voice of inadequacy was never silent, frequently prompting me to compare my flaws and failures to other people's strengths and successes. That negative voice was always there to compete for my attention and direction in life, and it still does; but it's not as loud and boisterous as it used to be. Still, I am forced to choose which voice I will listen and follow. People often view me as a natural leader with confidence to spare, but they have no idea of the internal fight I face every day to embrace effective self-leadership.

I've tried to make it a habit to listen to the voice inside that believes in me and my future success, the one that demands and expects the best from my attitude and actions. As I have followed that habit, I have identified some practical concepts, self-leadership principles, that help keep my own life on track. After interacting with individuals from around the world, I've learned that everyone needs such help. People often sabotage their own success, because they cannot lead themselves effectively. These simple concepts can make all the difference in the world.

I learned the value of these principles from the people who invested in the everyday experiences of my youth. They are self-leadership principles that my inner voice now speaks into my character every day. They continue to guide me through the challenges of life. I have had my share of hardships and disappointments, life is full of them; but these principles, help me move forward with confidence. They help prevent me from being my own worst enemy. Life is hard enough on its own, without my help to make it more difficult.

My wife, Lisa, and I have at times struggled financially, but we survived those tough seasons to experience an amazing financial turnaround. We now enjoy financial peace, debt-free living, and stability because of lessons learned in those early years. I battled grief for several years after my parents died. At my worst, I had no desire to live another day without them. I trekked through that dark period and arrived safe and sound on the other side because of these lessons I learned as a kid in small-town Georgia. What are they?

I had to develop a good understanding of real *success*, and maintain a clear picture of what it looks like for my life, the best "me" possible. I learned to *dream*, to see what is not there, yet. I learned the importance of a *right attitude*, to get rid of stinking thinking. I learned the value of *priorities*, to know what is important, and pay close attention to it. I learned the absolute necessity of having *integrity*, doing what is right. I made a commitment to keep on learning, growing, and to *finish* this life *well*.

These principles have been my friends through every step of my journey. My inner voice reminds me of their value and that they are always near to guide me in the right direction. They are not always easy to live by, but they are essential for real success, in my life and in yours. My hope is that this book will inspire you to embrace them and develop them as tools for your own journey. May they become your friends, too. Come along with me now back to Tallapoosa, Georgia for a short visit. As I reflect on the people and process of learning about success and self-leadership, I think you will enjoy the trip and be a better person because of it.

Reflections for Better Self-Leadership
- Identify the negative inner thoughts that discourage me, hindering my success. How can I work through those to lead myself well?

CHAPTER 2: LEARNING ABOUT SUCCESS

*Success does not chase after us each day,
but stupidity is in constant pursuit.*

I remember it as if it were yesterday as I walked the halls of the Tallapoosa Elementary School in Tallapoosa, Georgia, population 2,896. I can still hear the noise of kids chattering mixed with feet shuffling as we rushed to our classrooms before the bell rang. It was my own little domain. The rest of the world was like a fairytale, a place to be explored in a book and visited in my vast imagination.

It was the early 1970's. I had heard about the war in Vietnam as long as I could remember, but it was on the other side of the planet. My cousin Terry was there fighting. He served in the U.S. Army, and we often prayed for his safety and protection. We also longed for his return home. I was safe and secure, living in the same farmhouse and playing in the same yard on Riverside Road where my mom grew up.

It was a season of life I will never forget. It was simple, yet every day was an adventure. I started in the first grade in 1970. There was something special about the way the lunchroom lady, Mrs. Brooks, made those hot dogs. They were the absolute best hot dogs ever. The buns were warm and crispy on the outside and soft on the inside. I was a picky eater. If it wasn't hot dog day I took my own lunch, a peanut butter sandwich without jelly and peanut butter crackers.

The custodian, Mr. Cooney, often gave me candy. He was a special man and he made me feel special, too. I also saw Mr. Cooney each Sunday at church, and although he was an adult, almost the same age as my father, he seemed to have a special love for and connection to kids. Along with the candy, he even swapped Valentine's Day cards with us each year. While most adults drove a car from place to place, he rode a bicycle or walked.

I loved school. I played with my buddies on the playground. I had not been around girls very much until I started attending school, because I had three brothers and no sisters; but I quickly learned girls were not very hard to impress. At the age of six, I gave a girl a small toy car. She loved it and became my girlfriend for a couple of days.

I loved to ride the school bus. My bus driver, Mr. Doug, had a lot of tattoos and was a great storyteller. My brothers and I waited eagerly beside Riverside Road each day for the bus, wondering what story Mr. Doug would tell. Usually, it was some kind of hunting fable.

The trip to school was adventurous. We never knew what exciting thing would happen. On rainy days in the springtime, the bus would sometimes get stuck on those slick muddy roads, or a wooden bridge would wash away. Sometimes we saw deer eating in a farmer's field, or two kids would fight, and we would watch. Things had not changed much since my mom and dad were kids living on Riverside Road. Mr. Doug was also their bus driver when they went to school.

Once off the bus, I was off to see the wizard, I mean the teacher. But my teachers did seem magical like a wizard. I had some wonderful teachers in those early years. They were like moms away from home, and they seemed to know how to take me to a new level of understanding important things in life. In the first grade, Mrs. Littlefield realized I was a struggling reader who needed extra one-on-one tutoring. I can still hear her kind but firm voice saying, "Todd, you can do this!" She was right. I could. But I needed her affirmation and belief in me. She sent me a card and five dollars when I graduated from high school. She wrote that she was very proud of me.

In the second grade, I had Mrs. Cole. She was young and very pretty. She taught me how to write sentences and further develop my reading skills. In the third grade, I had Mrs. Kilgo. She taught me my multiplication tables and gave me a red fireman's hat when I learned them. In the fourth grade, I had Mrs. Morgan, and I had a crush on her. She had wavy blonde hair, a beautiful smile, and other than my mom, she was one of the kindest ladies I had ever known.

These teachers were amazing. If I had a question, they had the answer. I'm very thankful for them. They taught me the three R's – reading, 'riting and 'rithmetic. Without them, I would not be able to read my Bible, or anything else for that matter. I would not be able to write my name, calculate my ever-fluctuating weight, or balance my checkbook. The things they taught me were foundational for everything else I would ever learn in life.

I had a principal named Charlie Brown. Not many people have had that privilege. No, not the cartoon character, but the god-like character who was the boss of all the teachers and students while we were at school. He helped me begin to focus on success when I was in the third grade. He often came to our classrooms for a discussion about life. He organized the students into a circle, and then he would sit in the middle and ask us questions.

One day he asked our class, "What do you want to be when you grow up?" Now, let's get real. It was 1973. I was a healthy male third grader. Did I really have a choice? I would join the Army to fight in the Vietnam War, like my cousin, Terry. People would pray for me in church every Sunday, just

like we prayed for him. But suppose the war ended like everyone prayed? Well, I could be a fireman, a doctor, or help operate my dad's store, but I would really like to be a train engineer. I was told they made lots of money. My Uncle Chick had retired as a train engineer, and now he owned a brick house in town. Every time I had seen a train engineer he was sitting, looking out a window with the wind blowing in his face. He occasionally blew the horn to alert car drivers when nearing a railroad crossing. All those things sounded exciting. And who knows, while riding those tracks, I might even see some deer, just like on Mr. Doug's bus.

For the first time in my life, right there in the third grade, I began thinking seriously about success, and what I would be when I grew up. That question led to many more. Would I be good at it? Would my parents be proud of me? Would I go to college? No one in my family had graduated from college at that point. Could I really be a train engineer? Could I someday be President of Southern Railroad, or maybe even President of the United States? If I did something like that, I would really be successful, or would I? What did it mean to be a success? How would I know when I had achieved it?

Webster's Definition Of Success

Webster's Dictionary describes success as a "favorable result". Now that really helps a lot. Does that mean that eating Mrs. Brooks' hot dogs was a success? It was surely favorable, unless I ate too many of them. Certainly, it would be a "favorable result" to have a nice car, own a great business, and to have lots of money. I had heard people speak of millionaires as successful, but is every millionaire a success? If so, why do some of the wealthiest in the world live life secluded from others? Some have even committed suicide. How is that for "success"? Can success really be described with such things as money, cars, or corporations? These things, as with every tangible evidence, can be lost so easily. I was fifteen years old when I learned this hard truth about success.

A Tragic But Enlightening Day

It was a cold windy December day in the rolling foothills of the Appalachian Mountains in West Georgia. The cold moist air that settled over the Tallapoosa River seemed to flow up the hollow to make every room in our farmhouse feel like a freezer. Deer hunters and Christmas shoppers were hustling in and out of Wright's Army Store. Mom and Dad were the proud owners. They had sacrificed greatly to reach their dream of building a business of their own. I enjoyed working at "the store" every evening after school and on weekends.

I had an amazing life, and as far as my young mind could comprehend, success was simple. I had read the classic children's novel, *Where the Red Fern Grows*, and as a result, I followed in the footsteps of many boys who had lived in the rural foothills of the Appalachians. I purchased my own redbone hound and became a devoted coon hunter, chasing the ring-tailed critters late into the night. The coon hunting heritage had been passed down from the early pioneer mountain settlers who used raccoon fur to make clothing and its meat for basic survival.

I was the proud owner of a beautiful and awesome redbone coonhound, named Kate. I owned my own pickup truck. It was a 1969 Ford with a dog decal on each door. People knew I was in the dog business. I was the proud owner of Tallapoosa River Kennels. My first hound was a puppy named Bessy. Mr. Henry Lee Cokely, a big, kind, and gentle man with two gold teeth gave her to me. He was a good friend of my PaPaw Clark's. Bessy was a great dog, but she died giving birth to some puppies. A coon hunter like myself could not be without a hound. So, I emptied my three-hundred-dollar savings account to purchase Kate, a redbone hound like those in the novel, from my best friend Kevin's father, Douglas Campbell. He was the first real coon hunter I ever met. Tallapoosa River Kate was by far the best hound I had owned up to that point. As far as I was concerned, I had become a big success in a small town; something many say is impossible.

Kate had come from some of the finest redbone bloodlines in the country and a year after I got her, she gave birth to some beautiful puppies. Kevin's dad owned the father of the puppies. His name was Big Woods Chopper, and he was a "Grand Nite Champion," a title he had earned competing against other top hounds. He was an amazing hound, and I saw a room full of tall, shiny trophies at Kevin's house to prove it. Their trophy room wasn't highly organized, but to me, it was an impressive sight. Many of the trophies were taller than me. My plan was to raise and sell the puppies for one hundred dollars each. At last, I was going to be rich. What would I do with all that money? I could probably buy a champion coonhound of my own.

As the phone rang, I answered it with my usual enthusiastic greeting; "It's a great day at Wright's Army Store. May I help you?" I knew something was wrong when Mom responded, "Son, you need to come home! Something bad has happened at the kennel!"

"What is it Mom?" I asked, trying to remain calm.

Mom said, "It's Kate. I heard the other dogs barking. The dog house was on fire. I tried to put it out, but…"

"I'll be right there!" I said as I hung up the phone and quickly ran out the door.

I jumped into my truck, leaving customers behind, and headed home. My world was caving as a thousand thoughts, memories, and dreams flooded my mind. Surely success could not be so close and disappear so quickly, but my thoughts were about much more than money and success. Maybe Kate wasn't hurt too badly. I loved her. She loved me. Many times, we had hunted up and down the banks of the Tallapoosa River together in the middle of the night. We loved hunting with my friend Rodney Johnson and his Black and Tan hounds, Joe and Jack.

Many nights, Kate had made me proud with her hunting ability by tracking a raccoon to a tree and then wrapping her front legs around the tree and barking constantly until I arrived. And besides that, her amazing friendship was a special one. I've heard it said, "Every puppy needs to own a kid," and I was proud that Kate owned me. She even knew my smell. If we got separated while hunting, I could leave my coat on the ground where I had parked, and she would find it and lay on it until the next day, waiting for me to come back. A dog truly is a man's best friend. She never judged me or talked ugly to me. I was the most special person in her life. She was always happy to see me, and her sparkling brown eyes and wagging tail told me so.

As I arrived at the kennel, I realized a tragedy had happened and my life would never be the same. I had installed a lightbulb in her house to keep her puppies from freezing to death in the snow and cold. The wire had an electrical short and caught some hay and the doghouse on fire. She could have easily escaped the fire, but she refused to leave her puppies behind. Kate and her puppies were dead, and I felt responsible. My good intentions had taken her life and the life of her puppies, and I felt guilt and grief all the way to the bone. I wept uncontrollably as I dug a grave and buried them together. My heart was broken. I had lost an amazing friend, and my childhood dream was shattered. My immediate future was altered because of this sudden tragedy, but as I reflect upon that life-changing event, I have learned some things about "success" and life that I've never forgotten.

Real Success

Real success is not a one-time event such as having a good coonhound or being "set up" to make a lot of money. *Real success is not an event but a journey.* It's a journey that includes victories and tragedies, successes and failures, joys and sorrows.

Even our best efforts and intentions will often end in failure, tragedy, and disappointment. In such times, we must learn to forgive ourselves, others, and God for our disappointments. We must strive to use our God-given gifts and talents to the best of our ability, regardless of the outcome. We should live to have peace with yesterday, love for today, and a dream for tomorrow. We must work to earn enough money to provide for our family and to help others along the way. We must strive to have peace with God and to live so other people enjoy our presence, and to remain friends with ourselves. Life really can

21

TODO

be an amazing journey.

A life that reaches *real success* does not just happen automatically or by chance, neither is it a matter of luck. Success does not chase after us each day, but stupidity is in constant pursuit. A successful life must be lived intentionally. It must be carefully planned. Obstacles, challenges, and disappointments are waiting in our future to get us off track, but if we prepare for them, they will only add more adventure, amazement, and depth to our journey. Regardless of what is in our past, we can start today and make a beautiful, amazing life, but we will need to keep life in focus every day.

Many years have passed since that tragic but defining moment when Kate died. She was a true childhood friend with whom my mind is flooded with great and treasured memories. When she died, I lost a great companion and a great dream. Her loss forced me to deal with a very unpleasant part of life. A part of life I would experience over and over. Disappointment, grief, and loss.

A piece of my childhood heart was buried with Kate that day, and the heartbreak of her death helped push me into adulthood. Now my parents have died, too. And grandparents. And a brother. And friends. And many dreams. The Army Store became an empty building containing only memories of family and friends and great hunting stories. I have visited the farmhouse where I grew up. The towering oak that shaded the dog pen where Kate died is still standing, seemingly unaware of those events of the past. But times have changed. I have changed. That's not all bad. To my surprise, new dreams have been born and new friends have been made.

Recap

I left home on Riverside Road many years ago, but it was there that I learned lessons about life that continue to guide me today. It was there, on the same road where my parents, grandparents, and great grandparents lived, on a hill above the Tallapoosa River that the foundation of my life was built. Again, and again, I have felt the pain of grief as each of them has died, but along with the grief, I have become more aware that life is short. And I am more determined than ever to make every day a real success and to live life to the fullest.

As you join me on my journey, you will find that you are on one of your own. The details of our beginnings, cultures, values, and ambitions differ; but we can still experience the adventure together. The challenges ahead will be difficult, but the celebration of victory awaits. Success calls us. Our inner voice either cheers us on, or speaks words of discouragement. Which message will we listen to and follow?

To lead ourselves effectively toward success, we must develop some unique abilities – we already

23

have them inside us at some level. God put them there, but we must learn to use them with skill as we face the issues of life. The people who master their use will succeed. The people who don't, won't. Are you ready? Are you listening to the right voice inside? In the words of Mrs. Littlefield, "You can do this!"

THREE WORDS AND A KISS

Reflections for Better Self-Leadership
- Who has helped shape my thinking? Do I respect and admire them or is the opposite true? What have I learned from them?
- What significant event or experience in my past has affected me? What did I learn from it?
- How do I personally define success?
- If I could describe success for my life, what would it look like 20 or 30 years from now?

CHAPTER 3: DREAM: SEE WHAT ISN'T THERE... YET

*You can change the world with a great dream,
but you can hardly change your socks without one!*

What are your dreams? It's likely you have given up on some, and others stir inside you every waking hour. Some are simple and small, while others are massive and overwhelming. Some are new, yet others have been arousing your emotions since childhood.

Don't ignore your dreams!!! Yes, I'm yelling!!! Why? Because the pages of history are filled with everyday people who pursued their dreams, pushed through obstacles, and saw them come true. Every step forward for humanity has begun with a dream. The wheel. The automobile. The airplane. The space program. Modern medicine. And the story continues. I know, these examples are all inventions, but I assure you, each concept began as a dream. The quality of your own life and of the world are counting on you reaching your dreams.

The dreams inside us pull our life in a certain direction- to go to a certain school, work a certain job, live in a certain place, carry out a certain task, reach a certain goal, marry a certain person, experience a certain adventure or lifestyle. Dreams begin to take root as early as our preschool years. Ask any 4 or 5-year-old what they want for Christmas or what they want to be when they grow up, and they will be quick to answer. Dreams are already being formed that will shape the future of their lives, communities, and the world in which they will live. Now it's your turn and mine. How are dreams formed inside us? Are our dreams really that big of a deal? Do they actually shape our future and impact other people we don't even know?

Sweet Dreams

I shivered uncontrollably as I sat on the back of the hay trailer shortly before sunrise as Papaw drove the tractor. I could hardly move since Mamaw had me bundled up from head to toe like a mummy. I held on tightly for fear that my nine-year-old body might bounce off the trailer into the midst of the cows. A white frost, almost as white as Papaw's hair, covered the pasture grass. The cold morning air pierced the depths of my lungs with every breath.

My feet dangled as the massive black angus cattle gathered around me, pushing and shoving one another, hoping to get the first bite of hay we threw to them. In the frigid air, steam spewed from their nostrils and ascended from the fresh cow pies splatting on the frozen ground. We fed the cows before we ate our own breakfast. A farmer's duty was to take care of the animals first. Papaw said the only way the cattle could stay warm in such weather was to get their bellies full.

There was an unexplainable connection I could see between Papaw and his cows, as he shut the tractor engine off, sat in the freezing cold and watched them eat. The chomping of hay was the only sound breaking the early morning hush. Papaw was proud of his cattle. It was obvious they brought him peace and contentment, perhaps reminding him of feeding a herd with his dad or granddad when he was a little boy.

I dreamed of having my own farm with cattle someday, but I wanted horses too. Papaw was more of a practical farmer who would not feed anything he could not eat or plow behind. He had a mule and a tractor for that. Me, well, I was more of cowboy at heart, and a cowboy needed a good horse.

One of my weekly boyhood highlights was a trip to visit Mamaw and Papaw Bentley at their farm. We made the trip several times each a week. Their farm was in Muscadine, Alabama, just a few miles across the river from ours.

Mamaw had the coldest milk I ever drank, often straight from a cow that morning. She had the best pound cake I ever ate. I never knew her not to have some Wrigley's Doublemint or Spearmint gum in her purse. It was a regular treat for us grandkids.

Papaw helped create within my childhood soul

a love for simple things – country living, an appreciation for the past, and a commitment to have some fun every day. Those things continue to infiltrate my dreams. He was a big man with silky white hair. He was gentle and kind, and loved to laugh. In his presence, I felt special, like maybe I was a part his dream.

As a child, I was unaware that those experiences would be a primary tool to guide me into adulthood. And I was certainly unaware that God designed life to be lived that way, for our dreams to guide us. I have since learned that our future is impacted more by our ability to dream than any other ability God placed inside us. The capacity to imagine a better life, a better world, a better future is powerful. Everything great in our future begins with a dream in our past and present. A childhood dream is like God painting a picture of our future on our soul. And when we have no more dreams, our life is coming to a close. Even the Bible teaches us, *"Where there is no vision, the people perish"* (Proverbs 29:18).

The starting point for all our dreams begins with where we live each day. The people who guide us. Our experiences. The house we live in. The land, streets, and roads we travel on. The place where we live is the center of our universe. We can start right there and go anywhere in the world. Our small town or bustling city. Our trailer park, apartment building, or suburban subdivision. Our busy street or country dirt road. For me, it was Riverside Road, next to the Tallapoosa River.

Mamaw married Papaw after my real granddad, Claude Clark died of cancer, but Papaw treated my brothers, cousins, and me like his own grandkids. We worked in his chicken houses together. He taught me how to drive his truck and how to plow with a mule. I learned how to speak mule language as we plowed in the cornfield. "Gee" told the mule to go right. "Haw" meant go left. "Whoa" meant stop. A kissing sound signaled the mule to walk forward.

Wow! Just three words and a kiss. That was all the vocabulary needed to lead the mule. I was just a kid, but I could talk to a mule and he understood what I was saying. He went where I wanted him to go and did what I wanted him to do. It felt amazing to be so well connected to the big four-legged creature. And it may sound odd, but I loved how the old mule smelled, mixed with the smell of fresh plowed dirt. Learning to lead a mule was simple and easy. Learning to lead myself as I moved into adulthood would require much more effort and discipline.

After a hard day's work, we sat on the front porch each evening in the swing. I can still hear the squeak and rattle of the swing's chain. It was Papaw's favorite spot, and I loved it, too. We snapped and stringed beans and talked. Papaw told stories about growing up as a boy on that same farm. He told how, when he was a kid, his finger was cut off in an old grist mill where they used to grind corn to make cornmeal. As he raised his short index finger, he would retell the story I had heard at least a hundred times. I now wish I could hear him tell it again. Or he would tell about the rougher days in Tallapoosa when he was the police chief. His stories from the old days were often punctuated by the call of a bobwhite quail or a whippoorwill in the woods across the hayfield after the sun dipped over the horizon and the moon began to glow. And finally, if I was lucky enough to get to spend the night, I remember getting tucked into bed by Mamaw. Now, that was special.

As she pulled the covers up to my chin she would ask, "Do you know how much Mamaw loves you?" Whatever my response, "a hundred dollars' worth" or "a million dollars' worth," she always said, "More than that." Then she kissed me on the forehead and said, "Goodnight and sweet dreams."

Mamaw and Papaw are now gone, but those precious moments continue as vivid memories; and the words "Sweet Dreams" echo clearly in my mind.

The dreams formed in my soul in those early years are still alive and well. They continue to guide me on my journey.

Your childhood dreams guide you too. And the special people, places, and experiences of our childhoods will always be nearby to point us forward.

Our dreams about the future are like signposts that direct us toward the best life possible. Everything great in our future begins with one. Dreaming is an amazing God-given tool that is powerful and often affects our lives and the lives of others for many generations. Our dreams actually change the course of history.

Dreams Change The World

I loved hearing my dad tell stories about our family, stories that had been passed down from one generation to the next. Inside those stories were the dreams of my ancestors who lived before me. In the 1830's, several of them had followed their dreams to settle in the new wilderness territory in West Georgia, previously the Creek Indian Nation. In the controversial Treaty of Indian Springs, 1825, Creek Chief General William McIntosh, a Revolutionary War veteran, and two additional Creek Chiefs signed an agreement to sell all Creek territory west of the Flint River, so the United States could expand Georgia and the newly formed state of Alabama.

To most Creeks, the sale of the upper and lower Creek territories to the United States was seen as a betrayal, and as a result, they took the life of General McIntosh. His grave and plantation are now a Carroll County Public Park, just a few miles from my home.

The children of McIntosh became wealthy from the deal. His daughter moved to Texas and was the wealthiest woman in Texas at the time, owning a large plantation. However, for most of the Creek people, the transaction was a destructive disaster from which they would never recover. The land acquisition was beyond the point of return for the Creeks who, within a few years of the transaction, either left voluntarily or were removed by force to new Indian lands in today's Arkansas and Oklahoma. Many of them died on the journey, referred to as the "Trail of Tears," and many others spent the rest of their lives reminiscing and longing for their land of birth. The land where I now live.

It's a clear reminder that it's possible for one person's dream to become another person's nightmare. The same can be said of plantation owners and their slaves in the antebellum days of the Old South. Looking back on history should spur us on to be better humans, to dream big, and to treat others with dignity and respect in the process.

Most of Dad's ancestors with the names York, Philpot, Rowell, Eaves, Brown, Anthony, either received land grants in West Georgia for fighting in the Revolutionary War, or they purchased grants from veterans who did not want to move to the new territory. Either way, their dreams led them to settle on or near the Tallapoosa River in what was then Carroll County and today is Haralson County. My great grandfather Richard Baxter Wright came to west Georgia at the age of twenty-one, in 1881 from Anderson, South Carolina. He had heard about great opportunities in the region from his uncle Samuel Wright, who had followed his dreams there many years earlier. I have my great grandfather Wright's pocket watch and a small pocket notebook in which he wrote poems and kept records. He dreamed of having his own business and of raising a family. He saw both come true.

My ancestors combined dreams helped determine who I would be more than 130 years before I was born. The Tallapoosa River that had watered their crops served me also. I grew up fishing and swimming in the beautiful golden water, and hunting nearby, just like my dad and granddad. I often found Creek Indian arrowheads as a reminder of boys and men who once hunted the same woods and fields long ago. Rubbing a handmade arrowhead between my thumb, index, and middle fingers, I often stood there with mixed emotions. Grateful for a land that I loved, but aware that someone who loved it just as much had at one time left it behind unwillingly.

I was learning that the power of a dream is massive. You can change the world with a great dream, but you can hardly change your socks without one!

Many dreams never become a reality, but each one is a sign pointing us in a certain direction. They take us to the next step on our journey. Sometimes a certain dream just isn't meant to be, but it keeps us moving forward. At other times, it simply takes a while before we see the dream become a reality.

Getting The Cart Before The Horse

Following my dream of being a cowboy, the Western Ranch Edition of the Sears and Roebuck Catalog became a book I studied daily. It fostered and fueled my imagination. It was filled with the latest saddles, bridles, blankets, and other horse essentials. Most of it was more than I could afford, but it nurtured my fantasy of owning a horse.

I found a horse grooming kit priced at eight dollars. So, I began saving my money. I earned the eight dollars doing chores for a few weeks and ordered the kit. I thought it would never arrive. I had wanted a horse as early as I could recall; but Papaw would not buy one, and Mom and Dad could not afford one. Neither could I. But every day I imagined I was a cowboy, riding my horse in a full gallop, just like I had seen on TV. I dreamed of using my new hoof pick to dig the mud or small stone out of my horse's hoof after a long hard day, and using my new brush and curry comb to make my horse look beautiful. However, when it finally arrived, I had one major problem. I still did not own a horse. As a matter of fact, it was 23 years later before I bought my first horse; a sorrel quarter horse mare named Diamond.

For the next 20 years, I raised and trained several horses. I saddled up almost every week and went for a trail ride or a walk among my black angus cattle on my own farm. That dream never left, and it finally became a reality. I often wished I could invite Papaw Bentley to feed my cattle with me, but he had died when I was just seventeen.

I have now experienced the thrill of saddling several horses for their first ride. Diamond gave birth to my favorite horse ever, a palomino stallion I named Cutter. He was born in my arms, and I trained him and rode him for fourteen years until his death. Yes, I hit the ground a few times, but the joy of living out my dream from many years ago was worth any pain attached to it. I even paid to work on a ranch in New Mexico as a real cowboy for a week. And the relationship between my horses and me have been more therapeutic than a therapist could ever be. There's a cowboy proverb that says, "There's nothing better for the inside of a man (or woman) than the outside of a horse."

Through the years, I've learned that I don't accomplish everything I dream about, and neither will you, but we should dream big and often anyway. Why? Because no one ever accomplishes anything they don't first dream about. Every great accomplishment and exceptional moment in life begins with a dream. We never know which dream will match our character and God-given abilities to take us to the next step on our journey of an AMAZING life.

I Have A Dream

As I moved through junior high school and entered the eighth grade, I was pretty much the biggest boy on the school bus. My cousin, Donald, had nicknamed me Fat Boy and my mom ordered all my clothes from the "Husky" section of the Sears & Roebuck catalog. Since I was the biggest boy on the bus, I could sit where I wanted and choose who would sit with me. The bus was so crowded that several kids had to stand in the aisle until after the first few drop-offs. That provided a great opportunity for me. It was my chance to invite the best-looking girl on the bus to sit with me. She was only a sixth grader, but she was really good looking. I could not keep my eyes off her, and my boyhood brain imagined what she would grow into. I dreamed of her as my wife. Her name was Lisa.

She and her family had recently moved up to Riverside Road from the farmland in what we called the River Bottoms. I had seen her many times, but we had never really talked up close or anything. She was so pretty that she scared me. I got goose bumps and my heart raced every time I saw her. Some beautiful corn and soybeans had been produced down by the river; but she was absolutely the prettiest thing from the Bottoms I had ever seen. She had sparkling blue eyes, beautiful long blonde hair, and teeth as white as cotton balls. When I watched her walk, chills would run up and down my fourteen-year-old spine.

When I invited Lisa to sit with me that day on the bus, she agreed, but she kept her distance and ignored me, keeping her sparkling blue eyes focused in the opposite direction. I could tell she occasionally glanced my way. I finally got enough courage to say something, as my heart thumped against my chest. I reached over in a romantic move and gently pulled her hair to get her attention. I just wanted her to know she was blessed to be sitting in the seat with me, her future husband. I smiled and said, "I'm gonna marry you." She turned toward me and with fire in her eyes she said, "Leave me alone you greasy-headed fat slob!"

Wow! That did not turn out as I had planned, but there was something of which she was not aware. I had a dream. I was going to marry that girl, and I had told her so. But she was right about one thing; I was a greasy-headed fat slob.

What did she expect? I had been out hunting half the night with my redbone hound Kate and went to school after just a few hours of sleep. Sometimes I did not even take a bath before getting on the bus in the morning. Later, I'll finish this story, but for now let's think about the possible dream-killers in life.

Overcoming The Dream-Killers

The fact is I had some major obstacles blocking me from my dream. EVERY dream has MANY obstacles, and I had some work to do if I was going to reach mine. What was it about me that Lisa did not find charming? How could I fix it? What changes would be required in my life? What price would I have to pay? Was I willing to pay that price to reach one girl's heart? I guess I could settle for less. Would the value and happiness she would bring into my life be worth the changes I would need to make? Would I need to stop hunting and sell my dogs? Would I need to lose some weight?

That is the thought process we go through with every dream. Sometimes when we finish answering all those questions, we become discouraged. Too much change will be required, and the price is too high.

Discouragement is a powerful force that causes our dreams to evaporate. Discouragement can easily become the master of our lives, and it is a brutal ruler. When discouragement rules, it tells our hearts all the reasons our dreams cannot come true or why we don't deserve them. Discouragement is an enemy we must conquer and kill.

At other times, the people around us can be the dream-killers. They say, "Your dream is too big!" "You can't do that!" "You'll never amount to anything important!" "You will never graduate!" "She's too pretty for you!" "The economy is too bad to start a business!"

Sometimes, we simply are not willing to make the necessary changes in order to reach our dreams. It is too difficult and painful, and we see it as impossible. All of these are real obstacles we face, but we have only two options when it comes to reaching an AMAZING LIFE. We either dive in and try, or we quit before trying. We either watch others on their adventurous journeys of success, or we get up every day and take our own journey.

Every day, we have a thousand thoughts that appear and disappear like a bowl of ice cream on a hot summer day, but our real dreams continue to hang around in our heads and our hearts. After a while, our dreams begin to talk to us and tell us what to do and where to go in life. They become our own private tour guide, leading us through each adventure. They help us enjoy our journey. They keep us on track. Daily, they serve as a roadmap that gives us constant direction toward our AMAZING LIFE. It would be a good idea to write them in a notebook, a laptop or a smartphone.

Our greatest days of opportunity are ahead, but they begin with a dream. We've got to see it BEFORE it happens, or it won't happen. Great dreams are the foundation of EVERY AMAZING LIFE, but great dreams alone will not bring it to pass. They are only the beginning point. Reaching them will necessitate the right mindset and attitude, and any dream worth reaching will require hard work.

Does it sound like difficult days might be ahead? There is always a price to pay. Whether we dream of graduating from high school or college, getting a new job or career, finding a cure for cancer, getting a new car, or marrying a particular boy or girl, there is work to be done. We must dream big and work toward that dream daily.

Recap

Yes, the first essential tool for an AMAZING LIFE is our ability to DREAM. Life is the most amazing journey possible for those who chase their dreams. They determine where we go; yet again, there is no guarantee we will actually get there. However, our attitude will either help move us forward, or hold us back. The temptation to quit will greet us at the beginning and ending of every day as obstacles arise. Good thinking will take us to good places. Stinking thinking will bring us heartaches and disappointments. I learned this lesson the hard way.

Reflections for Better Self-Leadership
- List dreams that continue to stir inside of me and describe why they are important.
- What steps can I begin taking to pursue those dreams?

CHAPTER 4: ATTITUDE: LEARN TO DEAL WITH THE PROBLEMS OF STINKING THINKING

Our attitude is the fabric of our character, strongly swaying how we view ourselves.

"You'd better watch that attitude!", mom warned. I heard her snappy corrective caution anytime my youthful defiance approached being disrespectful. I deserved and needed the warning. She knew if she allowed a bad attitude to take root inside her "Toddy Boy" unimpeded, it would lead me to failure. She did not mean for me to actually "watch" it. She knew I had a bad case of stinking thinking, and she meant for me to correct it, improve it, fix it.

Our attitude is the pattern of thinking that informs our inner voice, and that voice then influences our every decision, behavior, and action.

Our attitude is the fabric of our character, strongly swaying how we view ourselves. It defines our identity and self-esteem. It is labeled as either good or bad. And we can all tell the difference between a bad attitude and a good one when we see it. Our attitude pattern is the reason we make *mostly* good or bad decisions, have *mostly* good or bad behaviors, "hang out" with *mostly* good or bad influences, and move into *mostly* good or bad directions in life. And while each of us has a baseline of good and bad attitudes that seem "normal" to us in our own personalities, we can choose, change, correct, and improve our attitudes. And we must because it never stays fixed! We must repair it over and again lest it sabotages our dreams and leads us into a life of disappointment. The resulting damage and frustration is painful.

I Quit!

I thought my heart was going to explode. The southern September sun felt like a blistering torch. I was hot and sweaty, and could not breathe. I was thirsty. I had never felt this way before. I had already vomited once that evening. Now, I was certain I was dying of a heart attack. Would my life really come to an end in junior high school? Then I heard Coach Cole command us to do some more sit-ups, jumping jacks, and pushups. I could not do a pushup.

The coach seemed like a nice guy during P.E. class each day. At the moment, he seemed more like my worst enemy. It was my first day of football practice, and he was stretching me physically, emotionally, and mentally far beyond where I had ever been. I was going to play ball for the West Haralson Red Devils. I had already asked one of the prettiest cheerleaders to sit with me on the bus to and from the first game. She said "Yes!"

I had dreamed of making great tackles, catching the ball, running for touchdowns, and of the cheerleaders fighting over me – the star of the football team. I might even get a kiss. I wanted one badly. I had never kissed a girl before, but I was beginning to think about it, a lot, like maybe once a minute or so. Oops. Better get back to football. Where was I? Oh yeah! I thought I was dying of a heart attack.

Instead of heeding Coach Cole and doing the exercises he asked for, I heard the voice inside me. "Football is too hard for you. You're not tough enough. You can't do this."

As my self-talk screamed for me to quit and walk away, I remembered that my mom was just a phone call away. Every fat cell in my chubby body seemed to be screaming for relief. My bulging belly had made the sit-ups difficult. I had obviously eaten too many hotdogs and peanut butter sandwiches in elementary school. My oldest brother, had survived football practice, and he seemed to love it, so I just did not think it would be as hard as it was.

Without giving it any more thought, I walked off the field and called my mom to come get me. As I walked, I knew I was walking away from some dreams that were important to me at the time, but, somehow, in light of the hard work it required, it did not seem to matter. Only two words came to mind: "I QUIT!"

There was great power in those two words, and it felt amazingly good when I said them. I soon got my breath back. It was a beautiful sight when Mom drove up to get me. She bought me a cold Coca-Cola and some potato chips and the pain in my body began to fade, but so did my dreams about football. My lack of determination left the gate open for discouragement to come in. When it came, my dream disappeared. Then I felt awful about myself. I felt like a failure.

That wasn't the first time I had quit something, and it wasn't the last. I had started playing the piano and quit. I joined the school band and played the saxophone and quit. I played the tuba and quit. I played baseball and quit. There were times when I even thought about quitting school. The twelfth grade seemed so far away. And college? Forget it!

I had developed a bad case of stinking thinking. I thought every activity in life should be fun and easy. If it became difficult, then I should quit and do something else. It's an attitude we all have to work through as we move from childhood to adulthood. It's a common teenage struggle, and it was a big one for me. Soon, it became a mental battle every time I faced a difficult challenge.

I'm not saying that we should never quit something.

I have heard some people sing solos in church who should have definitely quit. They seemed nice, but they could not sing and still can't. No amount of training can fix them. They simply are not solo singers. If they insist on continuing to sing, they should do so in a choir or the shower. The sooner they make that shift, the better off they and the people around them will be. Then they can move on to something at which they can succeed. So, quitting isn't always a bad thing.

However, too often, when a person quits something difficult, it feels so good it becomes an addiction. I did not realize it at the moment, but every time I quit something, it got easier to say those two words. "I quit." I needed a brain bath to get rid of my stinking thinking, and I needed it soon.

By the time I reached high school, I had begun to notice my pattern of quitting. When I was in the ninth grade, I decided to try football again. That time, day after day and week after week, I gave my best on the practice field. I did not have great talent and ability, and to this day, I've never actually played even one play in a real football game, but that year was a turning point in my attitude. I began to understand that sometimes life is going to get tough. I would need to force myself to move forward. Little did I realize how often in life I'd have to fight that same battle to find the determination inside to move through the pain. As I got older, I learned I was not the only person in the world who had to fight that battle. Everyone has to fight it.

Where There's A Will, There's A Way

My dad told me a story about his dad, Papa Taylor Wright. He had to fight a similar battle long before I was born. It was 1936, and America was still struggling to recover from the Great Depression, which was the collapse of America's economic system. My father was only four years old. His family lived in an old, rented log cabin on a hill above the River Bottoms, across the river from Riverside Road. Their house and everything they owned had burned a couple of years earlier, and they were starting over after losing it all. They were so poor their lives did not change very much before, during, or after the Great Depression.

Papa Wright was a country preacher and a sharecropper, but he had a dream of owning his own farm someday. He prioritized and worked hard to accomplish his dream. His wife, Mama Wright, did her part also as she walked seven miles each way to work at the cotton mill in Tallapoosa every day, regardless of weather conditions.

They had no car, but Papa Wright bought a mule and a new wagon for one hundred fifty dollars, which was a lot of money in those days. The mule's name was Roxy. This was going to be the year that he would make enough money to purchase his own farm. His dream seemed to finally be within reach. A man named Will agreed to help him plant and harvest about 50 acres of corn and cotton in the fertile bottomland soil, and that harvest would be his ticket to success.

During the spring and summer of that year, they labored in the field every day to till the ground, plant the seeds, and work the crop. Roxy and Will proved to be faithful partners in this journey. It looked as though all would be well, and they would have a bountiful harvest in a few weeks. Then the rain started. Day after day it rained. It rained so hard and so long that they could not tend the corn and cotton in the muddy fields. Grass began to smother out the crop. The river finally rose out of its banks and into the fields, causing complete destruction.

Shortly after that, Papa Wright loaned his wagon and Roxy to his father-in-law, my great grandpa Josh Rowell. He had barely left the farm with it when a speeding car came around a curve and collided with them. When the dust settled, Roxy was dead, the new wagon was scattered all over the highway, and Grandpa Rowell had a broken hip, causing him to limp for the rest of his life.

Papa Wright knew he had done his best, and no doubt he wondered why things did not turn out better. He, Will, and Mama Wright sat on the porch facing the reality of all the labor, time, and money gone. No doubt, they were on the verge of tears.

Then Papa Wright, attempting to fight the enemy of discouragement, said, "All my life I've always been told that where there is a will, there's a way." Then looking at Will, he said, "This is one time I had a Will, but there was just no way!" Then laughter filled the air.

That statement tells me a lot about Papa Wright and life. Sometimes life is going to feel difficult, painful, unfair and hopeless; but our attitudes either give birth to courage or discouragement. Just because we do our best, does not mean things will work out exactly as we hope and dream. During such times, we have to find a way to laugh instead of cry, to find the courage to face another day instead of becoming depressed and stuck in our failure.

Laughter brings hope and positive thoughts while crying usually brings sadness and a negative mindset. We are tempted to give up and quit during such times. However, just one year later Papa Wright planted another crop, and this time he reached his dream of buying his own farm on Riverside Road. It is there that he and Mama Wright raised their family and lived until death. Determination and the ability to overcome failure were of great value, and they will be of great value for us on our journeys as well.

Everybody wants to learn how to succeed, but the fact is we are going to fail much more often that we succeed. If we do not develop a rock-solid determination and a healthy sense of humor, we will never survive our failures and disappointments in life. If we don't survive our failures and disappointments, we will never experience success.

The way we think will determine how we face the good times and bad. Our thoughts lead us. If we don't learn early to think good thoughts, we are going to have a poor leader within. If we can learn how to lead ourselves well, we will have an edge on leading others.

Facing And Overcoming Fears

Another problematic attitude is the attitude of fear. Everyone is born with a sense of fear, but it is nurtured and developed further through experience. If you have a bad experience doing something, you are typically afraid to do it again. This is true for kids, teenagers, and adults.

As I entered high school, I remember being afraid of a lot of things. I was afraid of getting beat up by bigger guys, getting lost in the huge school building, and not being smart enough for high school work. Above all, I was afraid of standing before a class to give a speech. I had never given a speech before, but I had been told that once in high school I probably would have to do so. I was afraid I might say something wrong, or my brain might freeze up so I could not say anything at all. As I chose my schedule of classes, I was careful not to choose a class that might require me to give a speech. I took only the basics.

The class I was really excited about was vocational agriculture. It was a class about farming. I had grown up on a farm with pigs and chickens. Papaw had cows and grew field crops. I had come from a long line of farmers and people who lived off the land. I was dreaming of having a farm of my own someday. I was sure I could learn some things in class to help me in the farming business.

I remember walking into class on the first day of school excited about the one class I believed would actually be fun.

The teacher, Mr. McGill, walked into class that day and just messed up everything. He was a scary sight to a ninth grader. He did not really look like a teacher to me. He wore cowboy boots. He wore blue jeans that were a little too long at the top. They seemed to reach almost to his armpits. He had on a striped western shirt with pearl snap buttons. And there was something about the way he walked and looked at us that reminded me of a Nazi soldier. However, what he said was even worse. With his hands on his hips, he told us what would be expected of every student. He said, "By year's end, everybody is going to give a class speech on farming." Once again, I thought I was going to have a heart attack, and the words "I QUIT" immediately came to mind. Again, I still struggled with being stretched.

As the year passed, I became good friends with Mr. McGill, and he became one of my favorite teachers. I was sure that somehow something could be worked out, so I would not have to give a speech. However, to my disappointment, speech time finally arrived, and my name was called. My greatest fear was staring at me, and I was going to have to face it.

I actually argued with Mr. McGill and told him I could not and would not do a speech. He replied very simply, "Then I'll have to give you an F." So, I began to rethink my position. I tried to figure out a way that I could make this as painless as possible, get it over with and get back into my seat without dying or getting an F.

Mr. McGill, feeling my pain, asked, "Wright, doesn't your granddaddy have some cows?"

"Yes sir," I said.

"Then get up here and tell us about them," he told me. So, I did. With shaky knees and crackling voice, my first speech began:

> *My Papaw has some cows. They are Black Angus. They are black. I like to feed them, and I like to eat them. One of them ran after me one time in the pasture. I like them anyway. They are good ones.*

My inaugural speech lasted less than 30 seconds, but my two primary goals were accomplished: I did not die, and I did not get an F. It also felt really great to have faced and conquered one of my greatest fears. It felt much better than saying "I QUIT"! I had no idea that Mr. McGill was preparing me to live out my main purpose in life.

Just three years later, I was driving to college one morning as I prepared to be a mechanical engineer. A large dump truck loaded with gravel pulled into my lane, and it hit my car in a head-on collision. I was traveling at almost 70 mph, and, as it was happening, I was sure I was about to die. The car spun around several times and almost flipped over; but when it finally stopped, I was unscathed. However, my near-death experience caused me to think differently about life, and my purpose for living. God used that tragic event to lead me into a life of ministry, requiring me to speak before audiences every week.

Now for many years, I have worked to master the skill of speaking to audiences with courage, confidence, and effectiveness. The highlight of my life is to stand before national and international hearers and give life-changing words of hope and help. I've come a long way, and I continue to battle through my fears. And every time I step up to a podium, I'm reminded of my first speech in Mr. McGill's class. I am thankful for the journey.

Recap

Our dreams determine where we go in life. They will point the way to an AMAZING LIFE. Our attitudes must be carefully guarded, lest stinking thinking derails and destroys us. Our attitudes will determine whether we have the right mindsets to complete the journey. Without the right attitudes, we will quit when the journeys get tough, or fear will keep us from trying.

That's why we must identify our priorities. We must choose the things that are most important and pay close attention to them. They will help us make the hard decisions on our journeys. If we don't learn how to guard our priorities, our dreams will either evaporate or become nightmares.

Our dreams determine where we are going. Our attitudes determine if we get there.

Now, let's get our priorities in line. Our priorities determine how and when we get there. They help keep our dreams on track. We must determine the things that are most important and pay close attention to them. It is not easy, but it can and must be done!

Reflections for Better Self-Leadership
- How has a bad attitude impacted my life (maybe playing a role in hurting a relationship, destroying a career opportunity, or derailing a dream)?
- What are some good attitudes that need to become more prominent in my life?

CHAPTER 5: PRIORITIES: KNOW WHAT IS IMPORTANT AND PAY CLOSE ATTENTION TO IT

If it's my dream, I must make the sacrifices and determine the priorities to reach it.

What is the most important dream you want to realize next? Whatever it is will not cruise into your life automatically or easily. You must identify it and write it down, so you can then create a roadmap of decisions and actions that will take you there. It requires you choosing to do the things leading you toward your dream and eliminating the things that don't. This is the concept of setting priorities. It's not as easy to do as it sounds, but it must be done.

Achieving priorities always requires painful sacrifices and difficult decisions. There's a mathematical factor involved. Priorities require adding to your life some things that will likely be difficult and subtracting from your life some things that might be fun and easy.

All Dreams And No Priorities = A Dreamer

While in elementary and junior high school, my life

and dreams were settled and simple and seemed to be within reach. As I prepared to enter high school, everything was becoming complex and confusing. I had good grades as a student but was simply tired of homework and studying. I felt the constant pressure to perform. On most days, I felt inadequate and insecure, like I was not measuring up to my peers. I later learned that was a common feeling for kids at this stage. But, at that moment, I was tired of my confusion about the future and about life.

I sometimes dreamed of being a geologist, studying rocks, volcanoes, and dinosaurs. For a science project, I built a functioning volcano out of clay I dug from the riverbank behind our house. I packed the clay around a Coca-Cola bottle and used vinegar and baking soda to make it erupt.

At other times, I had dreamed of joining the U.S. Navy. My dad had served in the Navy, and a photo of his ship, along with his awards, hung proudly in our living room. As Admiral Todd Wright, I would lead my own fleet of ships to sail the seas. As I mentioned earlier, I could not do a single pushup; hence, my dad began to show me, so I would not be embarrassed at boot camp. By the end of the eighth grade, before going to high school, we were doing fifty pushups together in the living room floor a couple of times each week.

My dream to join the Navy was soon interrupted by my dream to marry that pretty, blonde-haired girl who sat with me on the bus. We would have lots of kids, cows, horses, and coon dogs while living happily ever after together on a farm. I wanted to marry her and join the Navy, but Dad said I should do one or the other. He said the Navy was not a good life for a family man.

Looking back, with all these dreams piling atop one another, I think I was just in a hurry to grow up and to get started with the future. I was a dreamer, yet I had no plan and no established priorities. I was not sure what do, how to do it, or how my life would turn out; but I dreamed of a better future. I wanted to be "somebody". I just wasn't sure who or what I wanted to be, nor did I know how.

Regardless of which dream I held at the moment, one thing was for sure, I could not move toward any of them without first graduating from high school, and that became my next major goal. So, I developed a plan and focused all of my attention on finishing high school in only three years, instead of four. Every other student would spend at least twelve years in school, but I was determined to finish in only eleven. That became my top priority, my most important dream to accomplish next. And as with every priority, it would require sacrifice, difficult decisions, and determination; but I was ready for the challenges ahead… I thought.

Fighting To Stay The Course

Sweat bubbled on my cheeks and was dripping off the tip of my nose. In darkness, with a welding helmet over my face, I squatted uncomfortably to weld some metal together for a school project. Welding was a new experience for me, and it made me feel like a man. I had started just a month earlier in my first year of summer school, between my eighth and ninth grade years. Mr. Mike Cohran was an excellent teacher, and he said I was a natural.

The odor of welding fumes and melted metal were unique, strong, and rank, but I would come to appreciate it. The temperature in the shop-type classroom was just short of unbearable that summer. It was also noisy with other students working on their own projects. Mine was to build new gates for the school driveway, and I took great pride in the fact that every person who visited the campus would first enter though "my" gates.

As I meticulously tried to lay the perfect weld, all of a sudden, my welding rod went cold and stuck in the previously molten metal. Only two things would have caused this - either my ground clamp had lost connection or my welding machine had been shut off. I lifted my helmet to look. The bright lights pierced my eyes, having become accustomed to the darkness. My ground clamp was still in place, but I noticed my machine was off. There was no one around it; so, I walked over, turned it back on, chipped and cleaned my weld, and went back to my task. I welded for a few seconds longer and it happened again. I looked up and again my machine was off, and no one was around. I got up and turned it back on. I chipped and cleaned my weld, but I had suspicions I was being intentionally sabotaged.

I started welding again, but this time after just a few seconds, I quickly stopped and lifted my helmet to look. There he was, a tenth grader sneaking around the corner to shut my welder off. And when I saw him, he snickered, as did a few of his friends. I did not like it. I was the target of his trickery. But, more importantly, the quality of my project was at risk.

I looked him straight in the eye and said, "OK, that's enough. Don't do that again." I thought he would say, "OK", laugh, and move on. To my surprise, he glanced back at the other guys, snickered, looked back at me and asked, "If I do it again, what are you gonna do about it?"

I swallowed hard, and before I knew it, I heard myself say, "I'm gonna beat your face in! That's what!" He snickered again and walked away. I hoped our confrontation was over. It wasn't. It was just beginning.

I had barely begun welding when it happened. I stood and raised my helmet only to see him standing there snickering. I said, "I told you if you did that again I was gonna beat your face in!" His long hair was parted down the middle. A few strands hung over his eyes. He blew a puff of air upward to move it. At the same moment, he tilted his head back and gave it a quick side-to-side shake. He thought he was so cool.

Several guys surrounded me and waited for the fight to begin. I was not usually a fighter. In fact, I was terrified, but I felt I had no choice.

Dad had taught me to never be a bully, and the preacher at Riverside Church had taught me to "turn the other cheek". However, Dad had also taught me if I was pushed into a fight, make sure I landed the first punch and make it count. So, while the bully boasted about what he was going to do to me, a little punk eighth grader, I laid one on him. Right in the mouth. Since he had braces on his teeth, it was not the smartest place to hit him. (I still have scars on my knuckles from that punch!) His lips and my fist were cut and bleeding badly. The other boys around us were egging us on. Blood spewed from his mouth onto both of us. He was furious, but before he could hit me back, I hit him again. He dropped to his knees, spitting blood. The fight was over.

From that point forward he never again picked on me. In fact, we later became good friends, worked side by side in a factory, and had lunch together each day. For a while, he even attended the church where I was pastor. He would laugh and tell others, "Don't mess with Todd. He will beat your face in." I had to admit to him that I did so out of sheer terror. We've laughed about our fight many times since, but at the time it was no laughing matter.

I could not let him stand in the way of my goal to build a gate for the school. I could not allow anything to stop what, at the time, seemed like such an important task. I was the only eighth grader and the youngest student at the high school that summer. I was an easy target for older, bigger boys. They could have flustered, distracted, or stopped me. But I had a goal of finishing high school in only three years. If I were to accomplish my goal, I would have to learn to deal with anyone or anything that might get in the way. And I did.

More Personal Sacrifices And Challenges

Finishing school a year early meant I had to go to summer school following eighth, ninth, tenth and eleventh grades. While everyone else was having fun during their high school summer breaks, I was in class. Once I made the decision and had gotten my parents to go along with it, I must admit that many times I questioned whether I had made a wise one. I had no idea how hard it would be to stay on track or that I would face so many obstacles.

My family had gone to the beach together every summer since my first- grade year. It was usually only three or four days, but it was the highlight of the entire year for us. Now, for four summers,

I would stay behind to fend for myself. And every year as my family went to the beach, my brothers were swimming and playing in the ocean with all the pretty girls, I was sitting in a classroom or doing homework.

There were many more obstacles to overcome. One summer, I had to drive to another city each day for school, thirty minutes away, because my school did not offer the course I needed. But I was determined to finish high school early. It was a priority that I had to focus on every day. This was my dream, and I was responsible for it. No other person could do it for me.

It was during that time that I learned a major principle I would have to apply many times in life. *If it's my dream, I must make the sacrifices and determine the priorities to reach it.* I should not expect other people to make the sacrifices for my dreams. And neither should you. Others may contribute, but we must pay the biggest price. Our priorities will determine if we really want it. Once we decide which things are important, we must stay focused on those things every day; and our dreams will soon become a possibility.

At some point, the principle of priorities must be applied to our daily actions and activities. If we do not plan our day, someone else will, and they will be focused on reaching THEIR dreams, NOT yours or mine. We must ask hard questions and make tough choices about our own days. What daily actions and activities will take me to my dream? What changes will I be required to make? Where should my focus be? What should I begin to do that I am not currently doing? What am I doing that I should stop doing? And once we answer those questions, we must focus on those things daily.

Moving up in life defies gravity. So, if we plan to go up, we can expect a struggle. It is easy to stay down. Gravity will help us do that. But if we dream of going up in life, we must get ready to pay the price. We must give up many small things to accomplish the big things we want to accomplish. It's never easy.

A Dream Come True

Do you remember that beautiful, blue-eyed, blonde-haired girl on the bus who called me a "greasy-headed fat slob"? The girl I dreamed of marrying? It seemed like an impossible dream, but doing so became one of my top priorities. There was a price to pay. I had to change some things about myself. When I did that, she actually called me for our first date. She invited me to go with her to a youth cookout at her church.

Since June 12, 1982, I've called her Mrs. Todd Wright. Believe it or not, she now calls me "Baby"! That's a long way from "greasy-headed fat slob". Yeah, I had to make some hard decisions. I sold my dogs, took a bath, lost some weight, and got a haircut. Now many years later, I'm not a fat dude anymore, even though I'm far from slim. And as far as my hair is concerned, I have none. I used to part it down the middle, but now there is nothing left to part. I'm as bald as an onion. At this point, she does not even care. She loves me!

I'm not sure when it began for her, but at some point, I became a part of her dreams, too. Now we are committed to helping each other experience an AMAZING LIFE. Many of our individual dreams are now meshed together. We've had our own farm with horses, cows, cats, and dogs. I still love to hear a good coonhound tree a raccoon, just like when I was a boy. In 2021, my coonhound, Grand Nite Champion, Silver Champion Better Legacy Squeak, won the year-long state race in Georgia, and was in the top 15 in the nation.

And yes, I did finish school a year early. I went to college during my senior year of high school. I went back and took part in the graduation ceremony with my class, though I had already completed my freshman year of college. It had seemed like a really important thing to do when I first made the decision in the eighth grade. Looking back, I'm not sure it made much of a difference. That's the great thing about hindsight. We can learn from it. If we're not cautious, we can look back and become cynical, frustrated, or even bitter about things that did or did not happen the way we anticipated. Such attitudes become poison that slowly and methodically kill our future dreams.

Recap

Yes, our ability to dream is the tool that determines where we go in life, and our attitude is the tool that helps us complete our journey. Our ability to develop good thinking patterns and to get rid of stinking thinking is essential. Our ability to choose and establish priorities determines if and how get there. An exceptional life requires that we use these tools skillfully, but there's another essential tool we must master: unwavering integrity. Our integrity determines if we will still like ourselves once we arrive. Let's keep moving!

TODD WRIGHT

Reflections for Better Self-Leadership
- What is my next, necessary step to realize my most important dream? When and how will I take it?
- How will I keep my daily habits, actions, and behaviors disciplined and focused toward my dream?
- Do I need to "give up" something that will hinder me reaching my dream? If so, what is it?
- What other changes should I make?

CHAPTER 6: INTEGRITY: DO WHAT'S RIGHT!

*Self-awareness, self-control, and self-correction
are essential to maintaining integrity.*

Integrity is the quality of being honest and having good moral values. We can easily recognize when a person has it and when they don't. It is at the core of maintaining credibility in every relationship, including the relationships with ourselves. We trust people who have it and we do not trust people who don't. *Integrity* comes from the root word *integer*, a mathematical term meaning a whole number, as opposed to a fraction. So, a person with integrity is a person who is whole and complete. Their life is not fragmented. The different areas of their life are in sync and flow from the same set of values. A person with integrity is not two-faced!

The 16th President of the United States was Abraham Lincoln. Physically, he was not an attractive man, and he knew it. However, he was known as a man with integrity, which was depicted in his nickname, Honest Abe. Supposedly, one of his political rivals once accused him of being two-faced. His response was, "If I had two faces, do you really think I would be wearing this one?"

No one maintains integrity all the time. We all have areas of our life with which we struggle to keep in line, and the challenges are different for each of us. Too often we are quick to identify the problematic areas in other people's lives and are blind to our own. We must be intentional about observing the attitudes and behaviors of our own lives and how they align with good, moral values. Self-awareness, self-control, and self-correction are essential to maintaining integrity.

Each time we cross the line to violate our integrity, our inner voice seems to record each scene and will surely remind us over and again of our failure. Not only do we lose credibility with others through our failures, we also lose credibility with ourselves. Sometimes other people will forgive us long before we forgive ourselves. And even after we do, our inner voice replays our failure, sapping our confidence, creating doubt, and making us fearful of trying again. The only way to repair the damage is to recognize our wrong, apologize, and make amends as much as physically possible. Doing so helps build a bridge toward restoring credibility with others and most importantly with ourselves.

The High Cost Of A Free Lunch

It was scary, confusing, and exciting all at the same time. I was in the tenth grade, two years before I had my accident and entered a life of ministry. My mind often reflected back to the third grade when Mr. Brown asked, "What do you want to be when you grow up?" Growing up was now coming sooner than I had expected, and it was more complicated than I had imagined. I was no longer a kid living in the idealistic and imaginary world of childhood, but I was not yet an adult either. I was in high school and still had no clarity about what I was going to do or be when I reached adulthood.

The Vietnam War was brought to a controversial close when I was in the fifth grade, so I would need to go to college and get a good job somewhere doing something other than being a soldier. Where would I go? What would I do? Could I be someone important? Could I be good at something that would cause people to respect me and be proud of me? Or would I fail and disappoint my parents and my teachers?

My favorite school days were not actually at school. My favorite days were the fieldtrips to the state Capitol, a historical park, a museum, electrical power plant, a farm picnic, a manufacturing plant, the FOX Theatre. These are just a few that I recall.

I remember one fieldtrip more than any other, but the memory is not really a good one. It was a two-stop trip to West Georgia Technical College and Southwire Company for an exploration tour.

At the time, I worked at Holcombe's Super-Value

grocery store after school and on weekends, bagging groceries and mopping floors. I was thankful to have the job, and I was making money. I was good at my job but confident that was not my long-term career.

I was now officially dating that pretty blonde-haired girl who I had wanted to marry someday. (Lisa wasn't old enough to actually date, but we sat together in the living room of each other's houses with our parents.) However, marriage was only part of my future. I would also need to have a career to provide for my family. I was still thinking of joining the Navy or becoming a mechanical engineer. Maybe both.

West Georgia Technical College and Southwire Company in Carrollton, Georgia, had an excellent partnership program that could help me get started into the engineering process as a machinist. The tour was great, and I experienced a brief moment of inspiration, imagining myself as one of the students preparing for the future.

Once the tour was over, it was time for my favorite event of every day - lunch. The teacher and bus driver decided to take us to Pizza Hut. We were instructed that students at each table would order their own pizza and would be responsible to pay their own bills.

As always, the pizza was amazing. When it was time to pay the bill, one boy at my table said, "I have a plan. Give the money to me, and the rest of you go out and get on the bus. Then, I will sneak out without paying and give you your money back." I knew it was not right, but it sounded like an exciting plan. I made the decision to participate in the scheme.

My heart rate increased as I walked past the cashier, out the door, and onto the bus. I had never done such a thing, and it seemed like every part of my body knew I was violating the moral code I knew to be upstanding. I was sweating like crazy. One by one, each boy at our table followed, and soon we were all on the bus headed home. We celebrated and gave each other high-fives as the bus pulled out of the parking lot. Just as he said, the boy gave us our money back. We had succeeded at walking out of the restaurant without paying, and we had gotten a free lunch.

The thirty-minute ride back to our school seemed to take longer than normal, and by the time we arrived, my brief life of crime was not quite as exciting as it had felt earlier. Something was not right inside of me. I was quiet as the school day came to an end. That evening, I wondered if perhaps the police would show up at my house to arrest me for stealing that pizza. The next day, I was afraid they would question me at school. One by one the days passed, and thankfully the police never came; however, I could not stop thinking about what I had done.

I had dreamed of being a lot of things when I grew up but never once had I dreamed of being a thief. There was a sick feeling inside of me. It felt like someone special to me had died, or I had lost my best friend. It was similar to how I felt when my dog Kate had died. Both times, it was the feeling of loss and grief but for different reasons.

I had done something that was contrary to the values I knew to be right. My values were the beliefs and principles for success planted inside of me by all of the respectable and successful people I had ever known. People like Mom and Dad, Mamaw and Papaw, the preacher at church, and my teachers. My actions would have been a disappointment to all of those people, if they had known.

Ernest Ingram, a mentor of mine, had once introduced me to one of his friends as "the finest Christian young man I know". I wondered what he would think of me if he found out I was a thief.

I had made a really dumb decision for a few dollars, and I carried my secret with me everywhere I went each day. In the process, I was losing the friend inside of me. But I knew life must go on. So, I did what my mom and dad had taught me to do at such times. I asked God to forgive me, and that seemed to help put the matter behind me... for a while.

As the years went by, my "life of crime" in the tenth

grade became a buried memory of the past. I never worked at Southwire, never attended West Georgia Technical College, never became a mechanical engineer, neither did I join the Navy. My journey, instead, took me away from West Georgia for a while. I went to seminary and became a pastor. I was helping people reach their God-given potential, and in the process, I hoped to reach my own.

Then fifteen years later, I was called back to West Georgia to be the pastor of Midway Church. Soon, I found myself sitting in that same Pizza Hut with my beautiful blonde-haired wife and two young daughters, preparing to have lunch.

I could hardly wait for a good slice of hot pizza. It was an excitement I had experienced many times before. Suddenly, I had a flash back to when my buddies and I had walked out of that very restaurant without paying. It had been many years since that event had even crossed my mind. I looked across the room and stared at the table where I had sat so many years ago and had made the decision to steal lunch. Now there was a voice inside of me saying, *Do the right thing!* There was another voice saying, *What if they want to press charges against you for your crime? Nobody knows about what you did. It's best to keep it that way.* Then the other voice said, *Do the right thing!*

I got up from the table and told my family, "I need to take care of something. I'll be right back." I walked up to the front of the restaurant, each step requiring extra effort. My heart rate increased as I approached the same cashier counter that I had sneaked past many years earlier. I struggled to get the words out, "Could I see the manager please?"

When she finally arrived from the kitchen, I handed her thirty dollars, and began to explain, "I walked out of your restaurant without paying, and I want to apologize and pay you." She asked, "When?" I said, "Fifteen years ago." She laughed and said, "I've only been here a few months. Don't worry about it. And I'm sure it did not cost this much." I said, "No, but it will help me if you will take this. Do what you would like with it." Then she thanked me for my honesty.

As I walked backed to join my family for lunch, I felt amazingly good on the inside. I had found the courage to face a failure and right a wrong. It felt like I had just renewed a relationship with an old friend. I was reminded that the most important friend I have is inside of me.

Now I needed to explain to my family why I had left the table for a few minutes. It was a great learning moment for all of us.

Every person in the world faces these moments. We allow our behaviors to occasionally move in a direction that is not in line with good values for success. We know we should do one thing, but instead we do another. Sometimes it takes longer than we imagine to clean up the mess that follows and to get our lives headed in the right direction again. Sometimes we never get back on track toward success. We get derailed and our life becomes a chaotic mess.

I wish I could say that was the last time I violated my integrity. It's a battle I have faced time and again. Most of the time I have chosen to do the right thing, but sometimes I have caved to the pressure and have done the wrong thing. The cleanup that follows is never fun. If you have such a mess from your past, the best time to have cleaned it up was a long time ago; the second-best time is now.

Values For Success

None of us has the exact same set of values, but certain values are accepted around the world as honorable and leading to success. These are values we must aspire to develop and possess. Values such as honesty, loyalty, courage, diligence, dependability, wisdom, persistence. From the time we are children, there are people in our lives who we learn from. They are people we respect. To us, they are bigger than life. They help define how we view the world and life itself. We love and respect them because of who they are, how they behave, and how they make us feel when we are in their presence. In many cases, these people are our family members, and we have no say in choosing who they will be. With the exception of choosing a spouse,

77

nobody gets to choose his or her family, and seldom can we choose our teachers. However, we do get to choose our friends, and these choices are extremely important. Their daily influence will either help us succeed or work against our success. So, we must choose our friends carefully.

Many good people are in prison or dead simply because they developed friendships with people who had destructive values. Others have experienced amazing success through the help of a friend.

At this point, there are several good questions that you should ask yourself as you continue your journey. They are questions I ask myself often, and if I answer them honestly, my integrity increases and so do my chances for success.

- Who am I and what are my moral values?
- Who should I be and what moral values do I need to change?
- What moral value in my life needs the most improvement right now?
- Are my moral behaviors being strengthened or weakened by my current friendships?

As you answer each of these questions, you will find yourself developing a road map to avoid the most painful and destructive pitfalls of your journey. As I look back over the years of my life, my greatest frustrations have been with myself. Too often, I've had to apologize for a wrong. Typically, it could have been avoided if I had only done what was right the first time. When you fail to do what is right, the next best thing is to be honest about your failure and do your best to make things right with the people you have hurt in the process.

My stolen lunch at Pizza Hut when I was in high school would have cost less than four dollars. Those four dollars of deception cost me many sleepless nights and robbed me of peace of mind. But more than that, it hindered my relationship with my most treasured friend - Me! I am grateful today that I have mended that friendship, but I have learned that I'll have to work to maintain it all of my life. Each day is filled with decisions that have the potential to destroy it.

Recap

Those are some of the lessons that have been most helpful to make me the man I am today. My look back in hindsight at the people, stories, and places that have shaped me can be uncomfortable. A different decision here or there could have harmed me or sabotaged my success in other ways. But it's also inspiring.

My dreams have directed and pointed me in the right direction. Correcting my attitude on a daily basis has kept me focused and determined to reach my dreams. Choosing the things that are most important and focusing on those priorities continue to keep me on track. And my commitment to do the right thing helps me tolerate myself and be happy with my journey.

As the hardships and pressures of life increase, our commitment to lean on these lessons as tools to help us must also increase. Let me remind you, success does not chase after us each day, but stupidity does! And usually stupidity sneaks into our life quietly and subtly with no apparent warning signs. We must make a strong commitment to finish well.

Reflections for Better Self-Leadership
- On a scale of 1 – 10 with 10 being highest, how do I currently rate myself on the qualities of:
    - Self-Awareness
    - Self-Control
    - Self-Correction
- Do I still like the friend inside of me? Why or why not?
- Is there a failure in my past for which I should make amends or apologize? How and when will I make amends?
- Who am I and what good moral values do I aspire to?
- What good moral values have I most often violated and need the most improvement in my life?
- Are my moral behaviors being strengthened or weakened by my current friendships? How will I correct this problem?

CHAPTER 7:
FINISHING WELL

*Without deliberate attention and
action, our lives drift.*

How old are you at this point? As I write this chapter, I am 57 years old, and likely, there are many more years behind me than before me. My experience has shown me that our lives, from birth 'til death, are like mine fields. At every age, season, and circumstance, dangers lie hidden beneath the surface, intending to sabotage our dreams and damage everything we treasure. We will never have enough experience, intelligence, education, nor wisdom, to put our life on cruise control mode and expect things to turn out okay. We must make an intentional commitment to finish each season well until there are no more seasons left to finish.

When I was a young man, I remember thinking that if I could reach the next major milestone safe and sound, such as school graduations, marriage, a new job, a new house, or a new baby; I could relax a bit. However, I would soon discover that concluding one season meant the birth of another. With each new season came new challenges and a new mine field with plenty of opportunities to self-destruct. I had to develop a strong commitment to finishing well in every endeavor, which did not come easy.

From Self-Sabotage To Self-Leadership

I was twenty-seven years old, and adulthood was much more difficult than I had ever imagined. Just ten years earlier, I had experienced my automobile accident, which had changed the direction of my life. Through the accident, God had clarified my purpose for living. He had put a new dream inside me, to be a pastor, but the pressure to perform every week, the high expectations of people, and the criticism of others were more than I could bear. I was going to quit my church and walk away from ministry altogether. My dream had become a nightmare.

I was feeling frustrated, flustered, disillusioned, and confused. I longed to go back to a simpler, kinder season of life, like feeding cows with Papaw or coon-hunting with Kate, but they were both gone. I could only go back in my memories. In defeat, line by line, I wrote my resignation, and I would read it to my church the following Sunday. I was a failure. I felt my only option was to quit. I just could not be a pastor any longer. Ministry life was not for me.

The ringing of my phone startled me. It was an untimely and unwelcomed intrusion as I sat at my office desk with my head in my hands, discouraged and depressed. Mt. Zion Church had been my first church where I served as the lead pastor, and it would be my last. It was a large church, with a private school, and ninety-eight employees. I had been the pastor there for only three years, but the challenges I faced were too complex for my inexperienced psyche. I was constantly being compared to my respected, seasoned, and confident predecessor. I also compared myself to him.

I was going to take Lisa and our two young daughters back to Tallapoosa, and I would help operate Wright's Army Store with Dad. No, that's not what I wanted, but quitting seemed like my only alternative. The pain was too great. I was surprised that the words 'I quit' still chased after me, even as an adult!

When I answered the phone, I was surprised that one of my seminary professors was calling. Dr. Billy Britt had never called me before that I could remember. He had taught my seminary class on leadership the previous semester, and I had great respect for him.

"What are you up to?" he asked.

"I just wrote my resignation," I responded.

"Where you going?" He assumed I was moving to another church.

"I'm going back to my hometown and help my dad

run his business. I'm finished with ministry."

"Hmmm. I hate to hear that," he empathized. "I was calling to invite you to a leadership training later this week with Dr. John Maxwell. He teaches some really great leadership insights. The training is by invitation only. About 30 participants. Some of the most successful pastors in Atlanta and surrounding areas are going to be there learning. If you will come, I will pay for your registration. Just hold off on your resignation for one week."

I had never heard of John Maxwell at the time. I hesitated, remembering that I usually felt more unsuccessful and depressed after attending such conferences, comparing my life to those whom I listened. Honestly, the last thing I wanted was to attend another training conference of any kind. Then for some reason, I said, "Okay. If you think he's really that good, I guess I'll go."

The following Friday, I drove to the conference which was hosted at a hotel in downtown Atlanta. I was the youngest person in the room. Numerous high-profile pastors were there whom I respected. They, too, were there to learn. I felt better about attending.

Soon, Dr. Maxwell came out, wearing a pull-over sweater, sat on a stool, and began talking to us about his life as a pastor and a leader. He seemed like one of us rather than an expert. He not only spoke about his successes, but he taught us through his failures. It was refreshing to hear him speak of his own flops. He seemed to have been as dumb in some of his decisions as I had been! He insisted we call him by his first name. He said, "I'm simple. My name is John."

As I listened to him, I found myself developing a sense of confidence I had never known. Up until that point, I had never really thought of myself as a leader. I thought I understood my calling as a pastor, but I had never seen leadership as a part of it. I had thought my job was to simply preach the Bible, care for people, and pray; and the rest would take care of itself. This new understanding, that I was to be a leader, was in itself worth attending the training. Then, concept by concept, John highlighted principles of effective leadership - Understanding influence, the power of a clear vision, how to share the vision, strengthening people skills, developing thinking skills, how to fund the vision.

Much of what I was learning was revolutionary for me. After a couple of hours, I became overwhelmed by the realization that God was not finished with me regarding ministry. To me, it seemed Dr. Britt's phone call was no accident. It was a divine appointment. I sat and wept in the room as I took notes, dreamed new dreams about ministry, and made new plans for the church where I was the pastor.

Perhaps the statement I heard that changed me most was, "YOU will be the most difficult person you will ever lead! Before you can lead your church or organization, you must learn to lead yourself!"

Self-leadership? That concept had never crossed my mind until that day, but since then, I've become addicted to it.

John explained how he led himself and kept himself on track in life. Among other things, he spent the week between Christmas and New Year's Day every year evaluating his life. It was a time set aside to see where he had been, where he is now, and where he was going. It was a time to learn from his mistakes, to reflect on his dreams and daily habits, to make adjustments in areas of his life that might be getting off track, and to set goals for the future.

A New Me

I left that leadership conference as a new person and a new pastor. I now embraced my new role as a leader, not only committed to lead the people and the church I was selected to lead, but most importantly, I was committed to leading myself. I tore up my resignation and threw it in the trash, which for me, was some bold self-leadership in action! I committed myself to learn, grow, and stretch. John provided a monthly leadership lesson that could help me learn and grow. I signed up.

I became a devoted student of self-leadership and organizational leadership, and that commitment moved me far beyond the hurdles and obstacles I had previously faced. It made me into the person and leader I am today.

I had come extremely close to quitting and walking away from one of the most important journeys of my life. I had almost derailed, and I was surprised at how easily it had happened. Stinking thinking had almost destroyed one of my dreams. Adulthood had its slippery slopes, and I had not even noticed the warning signs. I had made it through another treacherous minefield in life without getting blown up. Had it not been for that phone call ... wow!

Every year since that time, during the week between Christmas and New Year's Day, I have evaluated every area of my life, made adjustments, and set new goals. As a result, I have begun every new year wiser and with a clearer focus about my journey ahead. It's a process I'm committed to as long as I live. It has become my strategy to help me enter every new season, to stay the course, and to finish well.

I went on to serve Mt. Zion Church for another four years, my most effective years there. Then in 1996, I was called to become the pastor of Midway Church, in a rural community between Carrollton and Villa Rica, Georgia, where I have served for more than twenty-five years. We grew from two hundred weekly attenders to more than two thousand. In

2007, Midway was recognized as the fastest growing large church in the Georgia Baptist Convention.

During our time together, my character and leadership have been strongly tested as I led our 175-year-old congregation through much change. Our average age has dropped from 60 to 34. We have shifted to be a multi-racial church in rural Georgia. We have acquired, built, or renovated almost $15 million dollars of land and facilities and are free of debt. Through our local community and worldwide mission focus, we have invested millions of dollars to ease the pain and struggles of others and to bring them hope in Jesus. And recently, I launched a multi-year leadership succession plan to ensure Midway has effective leadership long after I'm gone. The succession plan is a part of my commitment to finish well at the church I lead.

Finishing Well

Having spoken at hundreds of funerals over the years, I've thought about the concept of *finishing well* for a long time, but it holds a higher priority today than ever as I prepare to wrap up my fifties and enter my sixties. I have a sense of moving into my final season of life. Mom died at the age of seventy-four, and Dad was seventy-nine. I pray God will let me live to reach the age of eighty-five, and if He does, that does not seem very far away at this point.

The childhood lessons I learned, principles and

tools I have written about in this book, continue to be essential for me and my future, just as they are for you and yours. They require intentionality. Without deliberate attention and action, our lives drift. As a result, life will become unruly, chaotic, and disappointing. And even if our youthfulness is filled with accomplishment, excitement, and thrill, something is seriously wrong if we do not finish well.

In 1968, just two years before I entered first grade to learn from Mrs. Littlefield, a slender thirty-two-year-old African man was boarding a plane in Tanzania. John Stephen Akhwari was flying to Mexico City to participate in the Olympic games, to represent his country in the long-distance marathon of 42 kilometers. At almost the halfway point of the race, he began to cramp. He tripped and fell as runners jockeyed for position. He fell awkwardly on the pavement, dislocating his knee and wounding his shoulder, but he got up and continued the race. Seventy-five runners had begun the race that day, but only fifty-two made it across the finish line. John Stephen Akwari finished last among them. Akwari completed the race more than an hour after the winner, Mamo Wolde of Ethiopia, crossed the finish line. When Akwari was asked by media why he continued to run through excruciating pain, with no possibility of winning. He responded, "My country did not send me five thousand miles to START a race. They sent me to

FINISH a race!"

His words deliver a good challenge for us. God did not give us life, put breath in our lungs, and dreams in our heart, so we could simply start the race we call life. We must finish the race and finish it well.

Recap

You and I are likely at very different stages of life, but we have the necessary tools to guide us to the finish line. A clear understanding of real success. Our dreams. Our attitudes. Our priorities. Our integrity. Our commitment to finish well.

I don't know what challenges we will face in the future, but I do know these God-given tools are ready and able to help us succeed. Thank you for joining me on my journey, and be assured I'm cheering for you on yours. I'll see you at the finish line!!!

Reflections for Better Self-Leadership
- Do I have the habit of finishing well at the things I start? How do I know?
- Will I make a commitment today to finish well with the relationships, roles, and endeavors of my life? If so, how do I intend to do so?
- What areas of self-leadership in my life need the most improvement?
  - Understand the meaning of a successful life
  - Dream, learn to see what is not there, yet
  - Have a right attitude, to get rid of the stinking thinking.
  - Learn the value of priorities, to know what is important, and pay close attention to it
  - Have integrity, doing what is right
  - Make a commitment to finish this life well
- What is the biggest improvement I will implement in my life from reading this book?

APPENDIX A: LIFE PERFORMANCE REVIEW

My Life Evaluation Performed the Week between Christmas and New Year's Day

THE OVERALL PROCESS
I. REFLECT AND EVALUATE
II. DECIDE WHAT YOU WANT AND WHY YOU WANT IT (What do I dream about? What are some of my goals I want to accomplish next?)
III. DEVELOP YOUR PLAN (Do I have attitudes that need to improve? What priorities must I establish to move me toward my dreams? Do I have character issues that I need to address? What are they?)
IV. TAKE ACTION ON JANUARY 1

FIVE (5) ESSENTIAL AREAS TO TAKE THROUGH THE ABOVE PROCESS

A. MY HEALTH (Physical. Mental/Emotional, Spiritual)
1. Current Weight
2. Current Challenges/Problems
3. Current Good Health Habits
4. Current Bad Health Habits

B. MY RELATIONSHIPS (Who's on the journey with me? How is my relationship with them? How can I make it better?)
1. Myself
2. God
3. Spouse
4. Children

5. Grandchildren
6. Mentors/Mentees- Who am I mentoring? Who is mentoring me?

C. MY FINANCES
1. Income Sources (Current? Options for Increase?)
2. Annual Income (Current? Options for Increase?)
3. Savings (Current? My plan for increasing my savings?)
4. Retirement (Current? My plan for increasing my retirement account?)
5. Giving/Generosity (Current? My plan for increasing my generosity?)
6. Debt (Current debts from smallest to largest. My plan to become debt-free?)

D. MY CAREER
1. How can I invest to make myself better? More education? Goals?
2. How long have I been with my current employer/business?
3. What has been my biggest contribution over the last year? Five years? Entire employment?
4. Would I be considered an "extra-mile" type of employee?
5. Am I being successful?
6. How can I improve?
7. What are some of my career goals?

E. SPECIAL EXPERIENCES FOR MY FAMILY AND MYSELF

1. Where have I been in the past year? Special Experiences?
2. Where do I dream of going? Special Experiences I dream about? How much will it cost? What is my savings plan for this? When can I go?
3. Where could I take the special person/ people in my life? Special Experiences? How much will it cost? What is my savings plan for this? When can we go?

APPENDIX B: PICTURES THROUGH THE YEARS

Easter service at the Coliseum

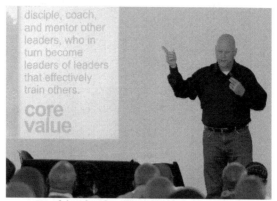

Teaching leadership principles in Africa

My first-grade teacher Mrs. Littlefield

Todd in Elementary School

Farmhouse on Riverside Road

My friend Douglas Campbell

Mamaw and Papaw Bentley's Wedding

My horse "Cutter"

My wife Lisa in 6th Grade

Todd in the 8th Grade

Lisa and Todd on their wedding day

Alfred and Dean Wright

My family

ACKNOWLEDGEMENTS

I owe a huge debt of gratitude to many for this book.

I'm grateful:
-for my parents, grandparents, extended family, teachers, coaches, pastors, and mentors for investing in my foundational years.

-for Zig Ziglar and John Maxwell, who improved my thinking and built my confidence while in my 20's, so I could become an effective leader of myself and others.

-for my wife, Lisa, who has been my constant cheerleader for over 40 years.

-for entrepreneurial leader, David Daniels, for his thoughtful and meaningful FOREWARD.

-for my friends Roger Alford, Dr. Anna Clifton, Dr. Wes Griffin, and Steve Schneider, who have critiqued and edited my writings to help this book become better.

-for Cameron Wilkins who designed the cover, Luke Hughes who assisted with the publishing process, and Dave Lanza who produced the audio version.

ABOUT THE AUTHOR

Todd Wright

 Todd is a Georgia megachurch pastor (Midway Church, Villa Rica, Georgia) and an international leadership conference speaker. He grew up in rural Georgia under the guidance and tutelage of sage elders who taught him crucial lessons in self-leadership. His upbringing was not unlike most other kids in small-town America, but through his skillful prose, he's able to take his readers to a simpler time and place, and describe the transformational wisdom he gained in his early years of life.

Todd is also the author of the self-leadership daily devotional Keeping Life in Focus: 365 Motivational Minutes and co-author of Journeys: Transitioning Churches to Relevance. He and his wife, Lisa, live on a quiet piece of acreage in Roopville, Georgia, not far from where they grew up.

Made in the USA
Columbia, SC
27 December 2022

75078521R00067